Goals
For The
Soul

LYNLEY DORNIER

BALBOA.PRESS
A DIVISION OF HAY HOUSE

Balboa Press books may be ordered through booksellers or by contacting:

Balboa Press
A Division of Hay House
1663 Liberty Drive
Bloomington, IN 47403
www.balboapress.com
1 (877) 407-4847

Print information available on the last page.

ISBN: 978-1-9822-4778-2 (sc)
ISBN: 978-1-9822-4780-5 (e)

Library of Congress Control Number: 2020913329

Balboa Press rev. date: 07/31/2020

Dedication

This book is dedicated to my son Bailey. I wrote this to you as a Life Soul Guide, to help you navigate your path of life. You are a gift. You have been my best teacher, my best gift, and what I am most proud of on this earth. You have taught me unconditional love, to forgive others, to laugh, to look for God in everyone, and to celebrate life. This life journey is yours, always know you have a home base and are loved. Your Soul Goal is to grow into the best version of You. We are learning everyday, until our last day on this earth. I am always in your heart sending love and support. I Love You to the Moon and back.

My Gratitude

I am grateful to all of my soul teachers who have showed up as a friend, family, co-worker, stranger, child, boss, pet, or patient. I am grateful to my guardian angels who have been my light. I am grateful to God, for showing me love is the way home. Love is all that matters.

Contents

Life

We are spirit living in a human body. We are spiritual beings. You are spirit-soul. The experience of life is to evolve your soul, to grow through human experiences, to your highest self. I believe on a soul level, I chose for my son to come into this life experience; as my son, and he chose for me to come into this earth experience as his mother. I am here as his teacher, and he is here as my teacher. I have guided and loved him, not without making mistakes of my own. I have shared with him I come from a place of love, and I try to bring my best self each day. When I do not bring my best self, I let him know I am sorry, my true intent is to bring my best self, and come from a place of love. I believe we are connected forever in our soul spirit, the soul returns to God, where we are all one.

2: Peter 1:5-9

This is a powerful prayer when you need help in life.

"And beside this, giving all diligence, add to your faith virtue, and to virtue knowledge;

And to knowledge temperance; and to temperance patience; and to patience godliness:

And to godliness brotherly kindness, and to brotherly kindness charity.

For if these things be in you, and abound, they make you that ye shall neither be barren nor unfruitful in the knowledge of our Lord Jesus Christ.

But he that lacketh these things is blind, and cannot see afar off, and hath forgotten that he was purged from his old sins".

2 Peter 1:5-9 King James Version Public Domain

Soul

Y our soul journey is your own. You are a child of God and perfect in who you are. This journey is yours, this is your life experience. The answers are all within your soul. Your soul is where God speaks to you. You feel your soul through that center place, your gut feeling. Go to your soul when you have a question, your soul/center will guide you. When you feel positive from your soul center about an issue/question, you know that is a yes to your question. When you feel fear, or negative feeling from your soul/center, listen to it, because that is a no signal, a red flag to look at the situation you are asking about. Learn to listen to your soul, this is where God will speak to you. Take time to be quiet, through prayer, or meditation, go to a quiet place and listen to your soul. I believe this is where god can speak to us. We only have to quiet our minds, and be open to hear the message. I believe our soul is spirit, and where we come from love. Our ego is our personality, our human part where we come from fear. The experience of this life is to learn to come from love, the soul, and not the ego-fear. *

*Seat of the Soul- Gary Sukav

Hail Mary

This is my favorite prayer.

Hail Mary full of Grace, the Lord is with thee. Blessed are thou among women and blessed is the fruit of thy womb Jesus. Holy Mary Mother of God, pray for us sinners now and at the hour of our death.

Amen

Forgiveness

Forgive yourself first. This is so true, and so important. Forgiveness starts with forgiving yourself. Forgive anything you carry with you. Forgiveness is powerful. Forgiveness is letting go of the hurt, forgiving another so you don't carry that pain or anger with you. Forgiving someone does not mean forgetting. Forgiving is letting go of the pain, so you can live lighter. Jesus said "forgive them for they know not what they do". *Luke 23-34. Some people in your life simply do not know, and are in a different place on their soul path. Karma always balances life, what you put out you receive. Forgiving allows you to continue on your path. You can feel anger, sadness, in the forgiveness process, and the emotions can come back and forth. Overtime the pain leaves you, and healing occurs.

*Luke 23-34 New King James Version

The Lord's Prayer

This helps to forgive yourself and others

Our Father, who art in heaven, hallowed be thy name;
thy kingdom come; thy will be done; on earth as it is in
heaven. Give us this day our daily bread. And forgive us our
trespasses, as we forgive those who trespass against us. And
lead us not into temptation; but deliver us from evil.
For this is the kingdom, the power and the glory, for ever and ever.

Amen

Kindness

Kindness matters. People in life remember how you treat them. I think kindness is the key to bringing humankind together. Kindness can be a smile, performing a random act of kindness for another, coming from a peaceful place to everyone you come in to contact with. Kindness is an attitude, and a verb. Each day, bring kindness to people in your day, and it passes on to others.

Glory Be

Glory be to the Father, and to the Son,

and to the Holy Spirit, as it was in the beginning,

is now, and ever shall be, a world without end.

Amen

Intention

Intention is your focused purpose. I think it is important to think about intention as it relates to a goal, or your life theme. I have created an "Intention for each New Year". I have created being more mindful as an intention for my year, to pause and be mindful about how I spend my days, and to live in the "NOW", the present moment. I have also chosen to live healthier, choosing one habit to be better at each year. I write down my Intention for the year, along with creating my vision board for the year. Giving the Intention energy, helps me focus on my Intention. I also focus on intention with work, volunteering or a goal. I ask myself "what is my purpose intention with this task? When you come from a pure-intention, the energy aligns with you and helps bring your goal into a reality.

The Miraculous Responsory of St. Anthony of Padua

If then you ask for miracles,
Death, error, all calamities,
the leprosy and deamons fly,
and health succeeds infirmities.

The sea obeys and fetters break,
and lifeless limbs you do restore,
while treasure lost are found again,
when young and old your aid implore,

All dangers vanish at your prayer,
And direst need doth quickly flee,
Let those who know thy power proclaim,
Let Paduans say: "These are of thee."

The sea obeys, and fetters break,
And lifeless limbs thou dost restore,
While treasures lost are found again,
When young and old thine aid implore.

To Father, Son, may glory be,
And Holy Spirit eternally,

The sea obeys, and fetters break,
And lifeless limbs thou dost restore,
Whilst treasures lost are found again,
When young and old thine aid implore.
Pray for us St. Anthony,
That we may be made worthy of the promises of
Christ.

O God, May the votive commemoration of St.Anthony,
Thy Confessor and Doctor, be a source of joy to Thy
Church, That she may always be fortified with spiritual
assistance, and may deserve to possess eternal joy.
Through Christ Our Lord. Amen.
By. St Bonaventure

Temperament & Mental Strength

Having a peaceful temperament and not reacting to others is key to mental strength. Training your mind to be still, and think before reacting is key to mental strength. When someone says or does something to get a reaction from you, go to that peaceful Soul Place. Remember, 'what someone thinks of you is none of your business', you can control how you react to them and respond to the situation. Sometimes, no reaction is the best reaction, because people like positive or negative attention. Mental Strength is staying soul centered. When someone is trying to get a reaction or response from you by a negative statement or act, you get to choose how you respond.

Prayer to St. Michael

This is a powerful prayer of protection.

Saint Michael Archangel,

Defend us in battle,

Be our protection against the wickedness and

Snares of the devil;

May God rebuke him, we humbly pray;

And do thou, O Prince of the heavenly host,

By the power of God, cast into hell

Satan and all the evil spirits

Who prowl through the world seeking the ruin of souls.

Amen.

Manifest Dreams

Think about something you want to happen, and it can happen. Your thoughts are powerful, be clear in your thoughts. What you believe you can receive. You can Manifest your Dreams, the Manifesting formula is:

1. Think/ Visualize what you want. Remember to be as specific as you can. Write it down, create a vision board. 2. See yourself there, as if it has already manifested. 3. Let it go. * See yourself releasing the dream to the universe. I always add to my dream: allow this to happen if it is my soul's best interest. You can achieve and have anything you can imagine, if you can see it, and add hard work to what you need to do, it can be.

*Shakti Gawain, 'Creative Visualization, 1978'

Abundance Prayer

From The Light of God that I am.
From the Love of God that I am.
From The Power of God that I am.
From the Heart of God that I am.
I Decree-
I dwell in the midst of Infinite Abundance.
The Abundance of God is my Infinite Source.
The River of Life never stops flowing and it flows through
me with lavish expression. Good comes to me through
unexpected avenues and God works in a myriad of ways
to bless me. I now open my mind to receive my good.

Nothing is too good to be true.
Nothing is too wonderful to have happen.
With God as my Source nothing amazes me.
I am not burdened by thoughts of past or future.
One is gone. The other is yet to come.

By the power of my belief, coupled with my purposeful fearless
actions and my deep rapport with God, my future is created
and my abundance made manifest. I ask and accept that I am
lifted in this and every moment into Higher Truth. My mind
is quiet. From this day forward I give freely and fearlessly into
Life and Life gives back to me with a fabulous increase.

Blessings come in expected and unexpected ways. Today provides for me in wondrous ways for the work that I do. I AM indeed grateful.
And so it is.
Amen

*Author unknown

Joy

J oy is happiness in your heart. Find joy every day. Create Joy in each day. Think of something that truly brings you Joy. Plan Joy in each day. Joy can be being with a friend, playing a game, eating an ice-cream cone, talking with a friend, being with nature. Find JOY in each day. This life is to be celebrated, to find JOY in the little moments of life, in the little things. The secret is to be looking for the joy, and the more Joy you will see.

Act of Adoration

O Sacrament most holy,
O Sacrament divine.
All praise and all thanksgiving be every moment Thine.
Come Holy Spirit. Come by means of the powerful intercession
of the Immaculate Heart of Mary, your well beloved spouse.
With these beads bind our children to your immaculate heart!
Amen

Children

Children are the best gift. Children are born through our bodies, and they have their own souls, and their life path of learnings. They are truly children of God, of the Universe. Children are our hearts with arms and legs. Children are our best teachers. Teach your children life lessons, pass on what you have learned as a soul. Guide them to live their dreams, their truth, their path. This life is their yellow brick road to follow. Love them, teach them to dream, to love, to find their passion in this life. It is their life path to learn. Guide their soul to follow their bliss.

Blessings of Mary

Our Blessed Virgin Mary, we ask that you
give us comfort in times of trouble,
We present to you our families and dedicate ourselves
to your teachings of compassion and love.
We ask that you make your presence known in our homes,
with our relatives, in our interest, and in all interactions.
Please take charge of them, and rid any activities
that may be displeasing to you.
Bless us and all our families, and help us never to offend your Son.
Please protect us from all dangers, provide our needs,
counsel us when we doubt, comfort us when we are
ill, and especially at the hour of our death.
We ask that you protect us from all evil, and allow us to
go to heaven to thank you, and together with you, we will
praise and love Jesus our Redeemer for all eternity.
Amen

Giving

"To Whom Much is Given, Much Will Be Required". * (Luke 12:48) Giving back is part of making the world a better place. Giving can take many forms. Giving of yourself, your time, your talents in some way to others. Choose a cause you believe in, give of yourself, volunteering, helping in some way. I believe we are here on this Earth to help each other, as souls we are called to help one another. We all come from the same soul source, and by helping each other, we help heal one another. My son and I enjoy giving through volunteering to serve the homeless at St. Vincent De Paul. This became our family tradition. I believe we have received more from the people we served. We have seen the love, the gratitude, the human connection in helping others. We are all called to help, to find some way to give back to humankind.

*Luke 12:48 King James Version Public Domain

Prayer of Gratitude

Blessed Mother I offer my gratitude in all the blessings
in my life, and I give to others the gifts of my spirit.
Amen.

Pain

Pain can take many forms. Emotional Pain and Physical Pain. Emotional Pain is felt at the core of our soul, and usually comes from some type of conflict, some hurt with a friend, mate, family. Through Pain some of the most powerful soul growth occurs. I believe there is always a lesson to learn through the pain. I ask "what is the life lesson in the situation:, there is always something to learn, to grow from the painful situation. I also believe asking for help from others is important. I have learned that having close friends/ family/ teachers or a guidance counselor/social worker is healing to share the painful situation. Unloading what is inside you, to talk about the pain and be able to release it is part of the healing process. I have learned sometimes I need to go outside the support network and talk with an advisor, a mentor, a counselor, a spiritual guide. I know from being a counselor, it is important to process a situation with someone outside of the situation, who can be independent, and give the tools I need to work out the situation. Be open to healing the pain through resources, support groups, a counselor, or an advisor who can help you. The Pain too shall pass, it takes time.

Physical Pain is usually some part of our body that needs healing. Be conscious that our body speaks to us in many ways. Our body can be telling us to slow down, or we are run down through a virus, infection, body ache we are experiencing. Pay attention to what your body is telling you; to rest, to eat healthy, drink more water, balance, release something. Your body speaks to you in many ways. Focus on how you feel, what area of your body needs attention.

What area needs rest? Your body, mind and spirit all work in alignment to be the highest version of your soul self.

The Lord is my shepherd; I shall not want,

He maketh me to lie down in green pastures: he leadeth me beside the still waters.

He restoreth my soul: he leadeth me in the paths of righteousness for his name's sake.

Yea, though I walk through the valley of the shadow of death, I will fear no evil: for thou art with me; thy rod and thy staff they comfort me.

Thou preparest a table before me in the presence of mine enemies: thou anointest my head with oil; my cup runneth over.

Surely goodness and mercy shall follow me all the days of my life: and I will dwell in the house of the Lord for ever.

*Psalm 22 King James Version Public Domain

Trust

Trust is something that is earned in others. Trust is built over time by actions. It is similar to making a deposit in the bank, when a friend is there for you, they make a trust deposit in your friendship account, when they break the trust, they make a withdraw from the friendship account. Time will show you if that person is trust worthy. Look at how full your friendship account is, surround yourself with people that deposit positive support and trust. True wealth are these people who fill your friendship account.

Share your dreams with only those who have similar goals or are one of the sacred friends. If you have a few people who you consider sacred soul friends, you are blessed. These are the soul friends who will always be there, and have your back. You will come across people who want to know your personal information to serve their own agenda. There are people who are only interested in their life, (takers, Narcissist). Know who they are, be nice, and keep them at a distance, do not let them in your inner soul friendship. **People will show you who they are by their actions, their words.** People can show you they come from Soul, a place of love and support, a positive place. They can also show you they are coming from EGO, a Negative place, jealousy, anger. Surround yourself with people you can trust, who fill your friendship account, people that lift your soul, people who want good for you, no matter what. Life is too short for negative people. Smile and be kind to negative people, and let them go on their path.

Trust Prayer

Holy Father, I come to you to bring me wisdom in

my heart and soul, to trust to know how to deal

with (name the situation) Holy Father, please

guide me to truth, and wisdom.

Amen

Career Path

Do what you love! Find something you love to do, something you are passionate about, and success will follow. Create a vision of your dream job, what would that job look like, what would that job feel like? Once you have the vision of the dream job, create a plan to get there. The vision is yours to create, it is your soul path. If you can dream it, you can manifest it! The formula is to create a vision of what job you want to see yourself doing, feel yourself in that job (as if it is already there), make a plan to get there, and the job will come.

Work Prayer

Dear Father,

Thank you for the wonderful skills and gifts you've so freely given me. I surrender all I am to you. Guide me on my path as I look for work opportunities. May I always serve you and others in the new adventures that await me.

Amen.

Gratitude

Gratitude is one of the most important actions to do daily. Each morning I start my day with gratitude. I think of 5 things I am grateful for, and before I go to bed at night I verbalize 5 things I am grateful for that I experienced that day. I found when I focus on all the blessings in my life, life gives me more blessings. What you appreciate, and have gratitude for grows. I find gratitude in my health, my friends, my family, my life, a beautiful day, watching a red bird. You can find gratitude in many things, walking the beach, being with nature, playing with friends, spending time with someone you care about. Focus your energy on what you are grateful for versus what you don't have in your life. You shift the energy of your life to bring more of what you are thankful for!

Gratitude Prayer

Thank you. I dwell upon the goodness in my life.

Thank you. I cherish in my heart your gift to me.

Thank you. I notice the blessings of life breath,

loving and sharing. I am so very grateful.

Thank you, Lord.

Amen.

Love

Love is the most powerful energy. Love is pure soul energy. When we come from love in a situation, it is pure, and from the soul. Love is the most powerful emotion you feel for others, and you must first LOVE YOURSELF. Start your day with Love to yourself. Loving yourself is the foundation for loving others.

SELF LOVE: Love thyself. Love yourself for the amazing wonderful soul that you are. You are here on Earth for a reason, you are enough just because you are here. TRULY LOVE YOU! Through loving yourself, you bring in and attract like energy to love. The light of God love is within each of us, for as God created us, we are all part of the same One-Love Soul, God. Look for Gods light in others, send love to others. You can send love by a thought or a prayer of that person.

LOVING A MATE: Loving another, a mate is giving unconditional love. Love is patient and kind, it does not control. Love a mate who is your equal; you have a friendship, a mutual respect, someone you trust, someone who makes your heart flutter when you are with them. Open your heart, and the love will come.

LOVE AS A VERB: Love heals all. When you put love in a situation, it is light energy that can transform a situation, or a person. When you come from love you are coming from your soul. Unconditional love is the best gift you can give or receive.

You are LOVED, you are a gift, you are an amazing soul spirit, living in a human body, with your own LOVE SOUL LIGHT to shine.

I Corinthians 13:4-13

Love is patient and kind; love does not envy or boast, it is not arrogant or rude. It does not insist on its own way; it is not irritable or resentful; it does not rejoice at wrongdoing, but rejoices with the truth. Love bears all things, believes all things, hopes all things, endures all things.

* I Corinthian 13:4-13 King James Version Public Domain

Gratitude to Blake

Thank you for guiding me on my Soul Path. You are an inspiration for truth, love, and kindness. Thank you for guiding me to share this book, to let each soul know they matter, and have their own path of life to follow. Thank you for being a Shining Soul. I pray your Soul Light continues to shine from above. You are love.

Prayer of Love

Holy, Holy, Holy Father, I pray you send light where there
is darkness. I pray you send love where there is pain. I
pray you send guidance where we are lost, I pray you send
wisdom when we are uncertain, I pray you send healing
to all souls, I pray you shine your holy light of love on
all of us, and we see your holy light in each other.
Amen

*Prayer of Love written by Lynley Dornier

CPSIA information can be obtained
at www.ICGtesting.com
Printed in the USA
LVHW090449181120
672003LV00008B/851

9 781982 247782